W9-CHS-165

Feast

By the same author

THE RED ENVELOPE

THE TAO OF WOMAN

Feast

by

CarolAnn Russell

Carol Ann Russell

Loonfeather Press
1993

Published by
Loonfeather Press
426 Bemidji Avenue
Bemidji, Minnesota 56601

ISBN 0-926147-04-8

This publication is made possible in part by
Region 2 Arts Council through funding from the
Minnesota Legislature.

for

Joyce Elaine

and

all the mothers and sisters

All life is your own,
All fruits of the earth
Are fruits of your womb,
Your union, your dance.

STARHAWK

Acknowledgments

Grateful acknowledgment is made to the publications in which some of these poems appeared.

Birmingham Poetry Review, Calyx, Envy's Sting, Iowa Woman, Nebraska Review, Poetry Northwest, The Poetry Review, Quarterly West, Songs for the Grandmothers.

Contents

Bodies of Knowledge

Sisters

Whispers

Sister, are you asleep? Are you sleeping?
We have been too quiet
waiting for visions, for the bleeding to stop.

Lying around the house
believing we were tired or sick
in the middle of the afternoon.
Voices tug at our bellies like silver hooks

threatening dead air.
Aren't you hungry?
In our dim bedroom, desire
floats like pollen. We can hardly breathe.
We have lost our color like a dream

we're ashamed to tell.
Come over to the window
and admire your breasts. Like pale moons
for years we have smiled at everyone
pretending like our mother
to write letters, rustling our papers

all the while sweating
silence
onto the blue-white sheets
ignoring the jalousies
clamped bitterly shut against
the shocking tongues
of light.

The Martyr

She's forgotten how to mind the store
her mother left her.
She dresses the window
in pink satin and hearts,
dead trees with plastic Jesus in a crib
and three kings in drag.
Her specialty is dismembering.
She works herself to the bone,
tries to stay a size twelve
while seeking fulfillment—
without food without love without lust.
Without knowing
she is prudent, unplugging
all the lights, even her own aura
in a storm. When the nuns
and the ideal housewives and mothers come
or the career women with their ladders
she is happy. Still and all
sometimes in the back room
she starts little fires.

The House of Dreams

Storm

A black horse in the lightning,
ragged vein of the world,
and rain,
its gray beauty
and compulsive kissing
until we are drenched
with knowledge of how things grow
thirsty, then fill,
then thirst again.

Lake in the Forest

Some travel here to die
and others to meet their monster,
hauling out the lichen-covered boat
to sail once more
into the eye of the storm.
Beautiful, demonic heroes of the past
gather on the terrace
to sip mint juleps
and creak in ancient wicker love-seats.

Shadow

There is more than one in this old house.
I think I saw something,
my double in a portrait.
I look around to see what's mine.
I am a gold-digger
come to find an ugly dwarf
banished years before:
she's working for me now.

Top Room

There is a door for every exit
and entrances which make a life.
On either side of the window seat
overlooking the circular drive,
matching closets wait like sisters,
one taller, whose ceilings slant
in opposite ways. I leave
the hooks exposed
and touch their brass knobs.
Beyond the bed another closet opens,
an invisible mother within
hanging up pretty clothes.
Behind the bureau some dust
quivers. It blows
toward the screened porch
through a French door
which lets in moonlight
staining clothes rumpled on the floor.

Fountain

Of all the handprints near the fountain
only one fits my woman's hand.
A white butterfly

quivers among leaves
and blurs
the prairie roses.

I hear ghost children
blowing bubbles
in the attic, steps

upon the stairs.
The purl of their laughter
returns me

to the fountain,
water spurting from gargoyle mouths
into a round pool,

and two small girls
holding hands
riding the stone lambs.

Resurrection

Returning from a bicycle ride
I enter a cool hallway
and find the girls
playing dress-up
with tattered fans.
One is black with half-gloves to match
and the other palest pink
flecked silver
through which a tiny eye
opens to a garden,
green apron of an old woman
crippled on her wooden chaise
calling to the sea
for the answer to death.
Now I wear the black mantilla,
tiara slipping backward
as we gaze into the mirror
and smile the smiles of girls
posing for the moment it takes the hidden light
to flash.

Swimming with Willow

I think of you and me floating out early afternoon
our feet in opposite oceans, arms
stretched to the middle west
until sunlight pools, glittering
in the warm dish of flesh.
Enter that mirror, that lap of water:
back and forth we go, mother,
daughter. Like an orphan
or a gilded scarecrow
I am swimming for my life, your many faces
at nine, thirteen and fifteen. We kiss
under the surface.
We fly in dreams like a murder of crows
toward each other
dropping ashes in our common soup,
dancing in the dark.
It is a lucky music that resembles
the sea. I stare into a cup
of saltwater, remembering
taking off our clothes on the beach
and surfing fat waves
always farther out where lips
of foam poised, imperfect kisses.
Below, our feet suffered the blackness.
On shore I etched a pentacle in sand,
an arm for each of us
and one unknown,
one ocean to make us over
in a phantom coupling,
a windfall of olives,
an owl.

Women in the Sauna

Like Renoir's "Large Bathers" we are
separate but linked,
concentric circles
of pink and peach light,
our bodies reforming
what space is—
the all, the everything
of flesh
casting off dark clothes
and habits

even the neat gloves
which kept us from touching,
thumbs prostitute
now part of the hand reaching out

to coax the scarred breast
and the mute vagina
to give up their stories,
tracing the spidery script on belly
and thigh,
the tiniest brush strokes

unspoken labor
spun again by the word
and the girls who slip in pearly skin
radiant with sweat
from the shadows between

us as we move
close enough to take turns
pinning up our dampened hair.

Gathering Pears

I crouch beneath the burdened tree,
the direction of harvest,
head bowed as though in prayer.
Cold sun glints off the crystal of my watch.
Blindly, I reach and withdraw
until pears glow, heaped on the matted grass.

The small basket overturns with groundfall
imperfect with wormholes.
The misshapen are altogether pears more than anything,
none the smooth line-drawing
that teaches children.

They smell of rain,
bruised, softly
counterpoint to late October.

Talking About the Penis

When it stands up they have no words
that don't say *love me*

and this is why they are blind to missiles,
guns, bullets, and bombs

the way they once dug blindly in the dirt
desperate for China, tunneling

snow and later
in the backseats of cars

slid their fingers like soft worms into girls
unaware of paradox and how they enjoyed

fishing with eggs and
slit actual worms with hooks

and plunked them bleeding in the waves
or in October cocked their guns

with something like love
and left their wives pregnant

with promises of fresh meat
and trophies—burnished horns and hides

to keep inside, proof they can control
the force called life outside their bodies,

that Judas, the implacable penis,
deathless, generous in its oneness

volunteering to rise and fall ten thousand
times a common life

good for nothing but to give
and then arrive and give again.

What "X" Is

Halloween, the festival of scars.
This time I know I'll dance at least twice
with other men.
I carry a check I'll never turn to money,
thinking about the whys of parties.
A friend, depressed from an operation,
her tiny body slit like a fish—
the cyst a gibbous moon,
paints my face: another mouth,
coral sprig and black
geometrical symbols marking the missing
moles, dark eyes,
periscopes of beauty at war with the sun.
We carve a pumpkin.
She takes the shiny aluminum knife
in her delicate hand and begins
to cut out the eyes,
working with the same deliberation as on my face.
I slice in the missing teeth to make it grin
horribly in the kitchen beside the Cuervo gold.
Rain comes down in fine needles.
I leave certain candles alone
and wear a hat. Life is tapping
its red shoe on the wooden porch.

Breasts

If we had touched them together,
if she had smiled,
slipping out of her blouse,
unfastening her white brassiere
would I have imagined myself
a mother someday
as I lay my cheek
against her rich and generous flesh?
Would I have fed myself then
against the world's starvation,
the ancient hunger for beauty
to shine its blue moon
into the cells of our bodies?

Skin to skin, loving women
in the sunlight of an ordinary day,
that singular language of touch.
Pinwheels of flesh leaf out
around the darkening buds
over the green fields of the heart,
keeping us rounded and soft
against the world's steel elbows.

I keep expecting things to change
into their opposites.
If and when the cancer comes
help me to remember
I am the center of that paradox,
my breasts the yin and yang
of pleasure, pain
perfectly paired and bonded,
the first part of my body
I touched alone,
and loved.
Now, pillowed against
the scarred chest of a friend,
her prostheses like burial mounds,
I am led to grow toward you
like some private miracle.

Waiting

In the clear afternoon
all the women I've ever loved
will sit down
and no one shall clear a thing away
or say it is time to go.
And our hands
with their invisible and visible rings,
hard circles of the past,
touch sometimes.
And light catches
between our fingers
as between lovers,
and glows awhile before it disappears.

White plates hold their perfect emptiness
like full moons
above the table in its skirt of linen,
near white with many washings.
The more brilliant and uneven
the smear of color which shapes each mouth,
the more we daub
onto starched white squares
a rorschach of remembering.
We toast the shrine of secrecy
one last, decent time
where over the withering years
a fat priest, that false mother,
has heard our confessions
for exorbitant price.
We wrap him in crocheted shroud.

Knit together like broken bones,
each amputation redeemed,
the scars become design.
So, when we ask in middle, ageless afternoon
for a candle for this table,
it is both to burn and to illumine:
the false last names of men,
those kindly, autocratic fathers
who fought for our right of beauty
and held us on their knees in our dreams;
the first, second, or third husbands
who gathered us into their arms
like cut iris
and wondered why we bled
before wilting into silk
and indelible scent.
These and the syllables of lovers
we pull around our shoulders
until the oriental print wavers
a landscape with human figures,
a house and garden,
a bridge we cross to the other side:
still afternoon, the jade water
rich with tattered lilies
pinned to the muddy bed.

Our infant selves coo, and wake.
We open our blouses willingly,
knowing what feeds
blesses with its stain.
The white cloth which we leave behind,
now rumpled and askew,
brushing the tops of our thighs,
is cut so that the corners
do not obliterate the center, nor the edges
folded twice into hems, then sewn—
the endings into air.

(for Hilda Raz)

18

Every Woman's Christmas

We cut the tree in our minds like the first snake,
and hang it with tinsel and our fears,
each in our separate houses, alone.

The ritual goes: turn beneath the mistletoe
and lose your soul. We do—happily,
then fasten the glass-eyed angel in white taffeta

mutely to the top. She sways gently,
erotic in colored lights, denying virginity
is a bodily state. Beneath her skirts

the invisible cave of her psyche admits
our thoughts. In moments, we have entered
and the room expands to let God out

while we women make the baby
and high on the burning tree
the angel rides wordless and free, winking.

WOOD '92

Mothers

Her Story

The photographs are black and white.
In a dress too dull to be anything
but brown, a watch pinned like a medal
to her flat chest, she frowns,
backed against the brick wall
of the world. It is 1938
and I can taste the fine dust of despair.
She will leave home, refusing to marry
the man her father has chosen,
and go to work. On a blind date
she will dance with my father
and say "yes." A church-bell rings
alone somewhere,
but she stays where she is.
How did she fly entirely whole
into the next photograph? Crouched
beside a greenhouse, in a white
dress with a barrette in her hair
she curves one arm around a baby
whose face flowers from the bonnet.
I find her when I look into myself.
I am her egg burst into skin and flame,
her tongue cut out at the farm.
I follow her every move
as she aches to read into my life
proof of the girl she left behind
whose mama feeds her children
on into the middle of the night.

Heirloom

Today I washed by hand the peach satin
embroidered kerchief my father brought
from Thailand before I was born.
It looks worn. A few threads have run,
I fear, beyond repair.
It has aged suddenly, like a face.
Like my mother's the year
I did not visit. Thinner,
imperceptibly graying as the maple leaves
die beside the lake.
I begged her for that kerchief.
When I was ten it meant everything
I didn't have. I stroked it
like skin. Buried years
in the trunk Grandmother gave
"for hope" she said
even though I eloped
and announced I'd never bear a child
but would go to college forever
and have real conversations
with people I didn't know.
Or love, I should have said.
Now, held up to the light
I see what it means.

Swimming Lesson

All winter and spring I swam with you
in the aqua pool
beneath the pines, the moon
of my belly waxing
as your spiral of light
curled around the fixed point
of my heart. Bound
by a red braid
we practiced the art of untying:
embodied spirit, body
spirited away,
upheld by the swell of water.

When children dive
they become something else, dolphin
or porpoise, slick with knowing
they will never go down.
The ocean moves
inside. Every Friday
the crippled man
leaves his wheel chair
to swim beside me,
slipping like a baby
into the blue. I am afraid
to meet his eyes.

I remember last autumn without you
alone in a room at the top of the stairs,
the water rising, how slowly
I pushed myself out of the metal chair
and began.

Labors

No one told me I would break into light
that I would drift awhile
and enlarge the heart.

I lit candles and steamed comfrey root
before you announced your birth-song,
familial moans between quick
breaths like a cat
in heat. Day and night were one.
The air-conditioner ran away
with the moon
and still the women rocked me
like a baby in their arms.

It was you setting fire
to my emptiness.
Your little boy bones pointed the way.
Harbinger of flood,
I crowed you mine in mother tongue
and you were. Promise
you'll call home
across that sound.

Fire and Water

Gulls fly up from the reddening lake
as if the waves had given birth
to wings. Nursing my son,
the tug of his mouth
and sweet milk dribbled down his chin
make beautiful the flight
of leaves. Their tiny boats of ash
glow with afternoon sun,
each with a miniature corpse.
My eyes water,
blue flames
drawn from the lake
I used to row across when I was a girl,
breasts asleep
beneath a cotton shirt.
I pulled the splintered oars
until my hands caught fire.

Lunaria

Crazy for the frogs to sing
I chop a hole in ice
and watch tadpoles churning
water into bloodstone.
I am green this winter,
watered by tears,
unseasoned as a female fish
who refuses to spawn.
I need magic to survive
the northern light,
some wild thyme.
But I am landlocked,
at the mercy of friends
who lose themselves in snow.

On the darkest day
I add a month to the calendar
and name myself
Queen of the Druids. If I could
I'd leave for Provence
and celebrate The Three Maries
with gypsies. Once
in the Green Mountains during a lunar eclipse
you slipped a silver hair,
a life-line in the dark
shadow of a lunar moth.

St. Augustine was wrong.
The blood I gather
mothers. I am
elm to your new vine
as silver fir and yew are sisters.
Alma Mater, you are all
the matter with me.
You laugh at sin
like the old woman who refuses
to die. Truth is
my son came with your tide
and sleeps, unafraid,
in pagan light. Your
natural history—Pliny be damned!
taught me all I know
of revolution: how to brighten.

Planting Cosmos

Gathering dust
beside the key to the antique clock

among bottles of Rioja,
you are anxious to be born.

All spring I have been planting you
in dream, turning the egg

of the universe inside
out, bathing in ashes.

The soil is good this year.
My catholic neighbor has placed

red and white roses
beside the statue of the Virgin

in memory of her daughter
flowering beyond the sky-blue robe.

My shadow shines
onto a bed of rocks.

After the chaos of ice
breaking up along the shore,

the lake has thawed,
washing up its kindling of reeds.

I seed your double light
in time to outwit frost,

a blaze of red and yellow
blossoming along the fence.

Midway Garden

You planned to bury the placenta
beneath a mountain ash
and I would keep the fountain going.
Everything bloomed
except the leaves of a pink poinsettia.
Ivy climbed the walls,
lilac swelled from gray bones
and poppies bled onto cotton tablecloths.
I painted my nails red
and joined the Unitarians.

When we stopped for sundaes at the Dairy Queen,
Midway Garden had a sign that read
"Open on Memorial Day."
We followed a teen-age boy in gold chains
to the aisle of trees: apple—
state fair and sweet sixteen.
The baby ate gravel.
I gathered up bridal wreath
and bleeding heart
for the dead patch out back.

At home in the garden
we take turns breaking sod,
rolling back each page of grass
to its alphabet of roots.
The baby plays with the green snake
of hose, washing his hands
in the spray. His face is flecked
with mud. It is Monday
and we are eating cake with midwives
while the sundial moves its shadow
across a stone frog.

The Josef Poems

Josef Napping

When Josef lies napping, swaddled
in flannel, spiders twirl
spinning their nets of silk.
When Josef likes napping, solemn as Churchill,
dust motes dance on the breath
of his snores.

Curled like a bodhisattva,
resplendent in diaper and tee-shirt
Josef presides: Prince
of the Boulevard, Sheik
of Changing Table and Tub.
In the middle of the day he sighs,

wriggles his fingers,
and waves his arms hello and goodbye
while his bare feet kick in the air
and his pink toes flutter. Pure
semaphore of flesh,
plumped in lambskin like Baby Genghis,

Little King of Piss and Drool, he
rules all that is real,
elemental, and free. Kisses
and poop are his subjects;
so are we. Willingly,
full of our deaths we live

for him, for he is the verb
of our household and when
he lies napping, we sing.

Josef Dropping Spoons

When the table is lit with daffodils
in their cobalt vase,
Josef will announce his intention
with gurgles and ahs
that blossom like blue roses
in a sultan's garden
until we have forgotten we are old.
Reaching beyond the sound
he finds the cold,
determinate spoons
at rest upon their simple napkins.
The first he raises into air

as if from the dead,
and in his tiny grip
it matters, mothering his sole
desire to influence the world
of table: scepter
to banish winter, and rule,
the shimmering spoon held high
as it will go toward heaven.
In the glow of his round face
he practices perfect
relinquishment

the second it falls
into the blue lake of linoleum,
a lure for the bones
of salmon, hook
for Kwan-yin who cups
all the abyss
in the shine of the kitchen
where swims a sperm
or a frozen flower
at home with the sun.

Josef and the Red Balloon

Like Akhaten he worships what is round
and red, a disc of the sun
tied to a hawk
at the back of his mind
hovering among the seven spheres
at war with none
alone in the power of the air.

A baby lonely for the OM
he babbles the mean
and tends the light within,
rising on tiptoe toward the shape of moon
whose sunburned aureole
he longs to kiss
as if he were Pharaoh
and she his mother Queen.
At the end of a soggy string
bobbing in the blue above

the all-seeing
pupil who sees what Isis saw
revolving in her labor,
a child of fortune
tethered to a carmine wheel
with wings,
a red balloon trailing
what is
minus what is not.

Feast

Having nursed my baby to sleep
on a rainy Saturday, wind
rocking the wooden bones of my house
until the windows groan,
I dream of Astarte
at home with pagans like me
who get pregnant and dance
on Sunday. Last night
I cracked her golden egg
into meringue, squeezed
the warty globes of seven lemons
to blend the sour with the sweet,
and built a ziggurat of pies.
It was a good Friday
for working magic. No time
for revenge, I bake for those I love
and give up all things Roman.
A stuffed rabbit,
ancestor of Oestre's moon-hare,
winks his green-glass eye, curled
in the arm of my sleeping son.
She is queen here and in her honor
we paint all eggs red. On Monday,
we will face East and mock
the Lord of Death frozen in his lake.
But today, my husband, a good bohemian,
will water his geraniums
and turn pancakes
yellow with cornmeal
in place of going to church
while I, mother of all matters
slip into purple silk
and have my own high-time
eating chocolate eggs and apples
while my baby snores.

Bodies of Knowledge

Dream of the Red World

I shall take up the gun which opened
your death and, cradling it close,
open my life with it: the steel door
of suicide unlocked and
the angel freed from her war with straw.
I shall take up the gun as
I take a woman I love to bed;
with respect that her power
matches mine, twin gardens and fountains
of blood linked by a stone wall.

Out of the bright envelopes of scars
sprout wings of radiant skin,
my secret sisters of the air, flesh
of my wandering. That dark
morning the vault opened, old father,
to take you into fertile
battle once again, I learned to fly.
You pulled the trigger against
my fear. The gun contains my power,
a family wand I learn
to empty, and to know who we are.

I take the gun of your dreams
and place it beside me, as I write.
Empowered by disguise, love
kills what it most desires. Open heart:
life opens mine. Death and you
slip out, father unforgiven, wise.
Together, we both survive.
As in my dream, I square the circle
of your wound and enter mine.
You cross my heart to keep, flesh and rune
I can read, bloody keyhole
I hold the skeleton for: old words
of blood and bone turning me
around to face myself. Queen I am
in the space between. Dead king
of my childhood, you bore the bullet
seed for my rising on wings,
then passed it, changed and golden, to me.

Turning the Wheel

Idol

After the tribes drifted out of touch
a hybrid woman appeared
wearing lion skin around her thighs,
elephant skin across her shoulders.
Because we cannot touch her
we say she had a child:
we mean we know her in the dark.

Ovulation opens the sky
and we are drenched in the wild grasses
of the pubic triangle.

St. Bride

Twins on an Athenian vase cursed us
with popular myth. Achilles
murdering Penthesilea
over and over until her sword
disappeared into a small wine cup:
the power of an unmarried woman
to be momentarily adored.

Opening and closing the lion's mouth
she is Banshee baptizing the hare
she is Alice with the white rabbit
falling down the hole.
This way the valley
can be entered, returned from.

Changing Woman

Go to the woman who was raped
and bathe her. Bring

her flowers, singing
of beauty old as the rain

and the water pitcher,
old as the menstrual washbowl,

the red water. Begin
the laying-on of hands.

Make a circle of stones
around the pool of her body.

Magna Mater

Drawn in dim light, a woman
crowned with tufted cap of a bird
opens her mouth
and moves 30,000 years closer than Christ.
Her limestone eyes resist
shadow. She is chewing a grass seed.

She could be the winds,
familiar voices
chanting our bodies of knowledge.
We could hold a mirror to remember.

Totem

I contain possibility, the bag
of happy-go-lucky
before the jump.
Through tunnel and birth canal
I connect joker and child.
In my open eye the embryo of now
walks on its hands, turning
handsprings through the world.
A tiny crocodile leads me.
A water lily grows
out of the stream bed, out of the lake
above the thought of snow.

Alchemy

First Dream

The soft spots on a baby's head vibrate like bells
when stroked by a human mother's hand. Truth pierces
the garden so that it bleeds secrets, fontanelles
of unfamiliar rivers in our private
Africas. Released by the vine of religion
we wander past soldiers near the skeleton gate
where earwigs of philosophy terrorize desire.
Off shore, the voices of friends and lovers:
Come into the water, they cry, their lives already fire
we will see by. The union of shadow and bone
seduces and, wisely, without sound something old
inside me swims heavily free and I go down,
dweller on the threshold moving toward the winged
awakening. Swallowed up like grain, gold returns to
earth: lapis of the birds and fish, you, me, everything.

Second Dream

I put on the gold charm bracelet mother gave me
when I travel down under the red world
and curl the cool reptile rope of its body
green around my arm, a live caduceous lifting
me on virgin wings over the pepper tree. Knots
unravel, leaving black holes and a sky drifting
when the snake in its fog of poison makes no sound
and strikes. Sudden as sex the fangs give up conscious
power and I the afterlife for this one wound
I can understand. Unlike the old torture of
paradise whose gold inflames the body with sleep,
snakebite plants seed in the fleshly garden of life
the body knows here and now. Now the queen's inside,
spiraled and alive, waiting for the king to spin
gold into earth, balancing that self-portrait, pride.

Third Dream

What I remember is your purity of heart,
how it struggled to survive the silk kimono.
Your weak back, a lyre for pain, played its double part
in the ordinary life we lived together.
At the edge of disaster, that immaculate
landscape of brother and sister, wind and water,
there is always the perfect picture, a window
through which one goes strolling to California.
Shedding kisses like old snakeskin, a diamond show
of death, the body grows imperfectly to love
the bloody feathers of its paradox. Speechless
and radiant and self-contained as flesh, dream dives
into the crystal sea, clotting your heart's blood with mine.
Garnet of the backward glance, the double heart beats
in the ghost house, gem in the vault of sleep, a sign.

Fourth Dream

One day, lured by a dragon in tourmaline sea,
I stop gathering seed and call to the mermaids
burning in blue-green flames, tiny origami
wings which carried them in time to my lover's side.
A calm skin takes their place, blue, womanly, and wise,
a mantle flung over the deep and secret bride.
When I reach her, she has fallen asleep, rocking
gently among the rocks. A run-down beach house
on the coral sand holds an old woman hawking
the pink and peach shells of the deep, labial
but toothless as she. Thinking to buy, I fail to
see the world tilting outside its wall, alluvial
moonlit gash, wooden leg pushed by the sky's blue knife.
Where I am, money in hand, the floor is water,
quicksilver, safe womb for the wave-scarred, pregnant life.

Fifth Dream

Head first into the world the child arrives, bloodied
by the only eternity it knows, cavern
of bones and mother's milk. Its eyes silver and muddied
from seeing within, go blind for a time, backward
into the hospital grave. Grace returns the child
imperfect, inconsolable from going downward
against its will, home to the wooden house of life
whose back garden blooms with lapis, lies, and poppies.
Wild body gentles the mind's ghost into belief
no amends will change, nor the castle walls caved in
from saving, nor the wicker cradle empty of
song. Mothers have always known to spend the coffin
on the young who fill it with material dreams, sperm,
and music the cicadas make against the cold.

How a Child Comes into This World

The dark bird dives into the heart
without knowing
what it wants. It hungers
for another pair
of wings, a woman flying
on a trapeze above the moonlit dust
in a dying circus. This
is a foreign country, earth
with traffic and seeds.
Only the child knows
the question
the bird
and the woman
breathe together
in their dream of grass
awakening. Between,
the image flickers
with a mouth of flame
fed by an angel in black and white
who longs for skin
again, to touch
and kiss
the mystery he feared
would swallow him
back to the child
and the red sleeve
from which he took flight.

And so the woman flies for him
each night, above faces
of strangers
who have forgotten their bodies,
where they came from.
Children of desire, all
orphans holding each blade
of grass to the hillside
remembering when birds
were song
and the heart was a field
swept clean by wings,
now looking up as the woman
lets go
and the bird disappears.

(from the painting, *Feast on the Earth,*
by Nadema Agaard-Smith)

CarolAnn Russell

Poet

CarolAnn Russell's book of poems, *The Red Envelope*, University Presses of Florida (1985), entered its second printing in Spring 1991. The poet Lazaro Lima is currently completing the Spanish translation, *El sobre colorado*. About that manuscript, critic Charles Guenther *(St. Louis Post-Dispatch)* said, "One of the finest first books of poetry I've read in years. . .Both intensely personal and impersonal, her poems are broad and profound, with uncanny vision." Critic Jonathan Holden describes her work as possessing "unfamiliar eloquence." A chapbook, *The TAO of Woman*, published by Loonfeather Press in September 1991, entered its second printing in 1992. Her poems have also appeared in many small press magazines and journals, including *Poetry Northwest, Colorado Review, Poet & Critic, Ploughshares* and *Ohio Review*. She has been anthologized in *Midwest Poets, Alternatives, Men and Women, Northwest Poets, Decade Dance*, and others.

Since 1977, CarolAnn has been the recipient of nine literary awards, including the Academy of American Poets, Poetry Society of America, Pacific Northwest Writers Conference, and Lake Superior Writers Series. She has received grants and fellowships from Ragdale Foundation, Southern Connecticut State University, Northwest Area Foundation, University of Montana, Bemidji State University, National Endowment for the Arts, and others. She regularly reads at universities, conferences, and in communities. She is a member of P.E.N. and the Associated Writing Programs.

In 1989, CarolAnn directed the Headwaters Writers Conference, Itasca State Park, and she has sat on the editorial boards of a number of literary journals, including *Giltedge* and *Cutbank*. She has a Ph.D. in Creative Writing from the University of Nebraska and is an associate professor of English at Bemidji State University, where she teaches creative writing and women's studies, and directs the Different Drummers reading series. She lives with her husband, Michael Schlemper, an artist, and their son, Josef, on lake Bemidji.

These are sensual poems—womanly
and wise. In this superb collection,
filled with startling and unexpected
images, CarolAnn Russell writes
about motherhood, marriage, and
sisterly love. The female figures are
legendary in stature—

Marcia Southwick